I LIKE YOUR TENACITY

30 Anthems to Stir Up Hope in
The Middle of Disappointment

Olivia Alnes

INTRODUCTION

Have you ever been soul-crushingly disappointed?

Maybe the relationship you thought was forever is over. Maybe you failed a class that was required to graduate with your desired major. Maybe someone you trusted betrayed you. Maybe your dream job led to burn out. Maybe you prayed for healing but sickness still prevailed. Maybe someone you loved died.

For me, one of the most soul-crushing disappointments in my life came in the form of unanswered prayers.

At the end of high school, my parents' marriage was pretty shakey. I started praying for a miracle while feeling so afraid to talk to people about the issue. When I finally started opening up to friends and mentors in college, hope was stirred up in my spirit. Sitting on my floral quilt in my freshman dorm room, I believed for the first time that God could restore my parent's marriage.

Less than a year later, everything fell apart.

Two years after that, they got a divorce.

When I hit the five year mark of praying for my family, I was exhausted. It was so hard to believe that God was good when it felt like things kept getting worse, even long after the ink on the divorce papers had dried. It felt like a death that we were living on repeat.

Disappointment sunk in.

I was disappointed that I couldn't do anything to fix the situation. I was disappointed in the results. I was disappointed in life. I was disappointed in God.

Disappointment wanted to tell the story.

Today, my relationship with hope and disappointment looks wildly different.

The situation hasn't changed and sometimes, it seems to be worse than ever before, yet it doesn't feel hopeless. I don't feel defeated. I feel strong and tender, sad and hopeful, expectant and surrendered.

What has changed is tenacity.

God led me through a process of becoming tenacious.

Tenacious means to be "persistent in maintaining, adhering to, or seeking something valued or desired" (Merriam-Webster.com). Tenacity is perseverance, holding on tight with all you've got, and the courage to keep going.

Tenacity is required to not only change the world, but to thrive in it.

You will face hard things. You will experience disappointment ranging from a bad day to complete heartbreak. What you need deep within is the ability to keep going when you don't want to. You need to learn how to stir up hope. You need the ability to hold on.

There is breakthrough coming. While Jesus never promised us an easy life, the Bible is stuffed to the brim with promises about God delivering and rescuing us. The hope that I'm offering you in these words won't come from me or even inside of you. This hope is only made possible with a good, kind God.

These 30 Days are an invitation to experience that good, kind God. Whether it's for the first time or the thousandth time, you are so close to one moment with God that can change everything.

Knowing, experiencing, and being radically loved by Him will spark hope in a way that nothing else can.

Let's go! Let's dive in! We are in this together.

Be brave. Be strong.
Don't give up.
Expect God to get here soon.
Psalms 31:24 MSG

BEFORE WE START, A QUICK NOTE:

I want you to picture us curled up on the couch with big mugs of coffee or tea in our hands. We're hashing out the hard things in life as we hold the heavy and light together. There's space for you to be yourself and let the walls down as we trade stories back and forth.

While this might feel like a one-sided conversation, know that if we were in person, there'd be plenty of listening on my part. The power of presence is something I believe in.

This is why I want you to know that this is a safe place.

Come as your full self – with your hopes and dreams and disappointments. Come with your frustrations. Come with your hurt. Come with your joys and celebrations. Come with your confusion. Come would your doubts. Come with your cynicism and wonder and fear and excitement. Come as you are.

You belong here.

HOW TO USE THIS DEVOTIONAL

Each day is meant to jumpstart connection with Jesus, yourself, and others. The "Going Deeper" section provides you with next steps to make the message your own. You're going to want a journal and maybe a trusted friend to help you process.

Going Deeper Includes:
Scripture – each day will end with a passage from the Bible. I'd encourage you to read slowly and let it sink in. You can also grab your Bible and read the context surrounding the verse.

Ask – spend some time thinking about this question and use it as a journal prompt or discussion starter (there is a full list of discussion questions in the back as well).

Anthem – say these words out loud as an affirmation and declaration of truth. You can even write them down and post them around your home, vehicle, workspace, etc – wherever you most need to see them!

Activate – this is your chance to take action on what you've read. Often this is a journal activity or a specific way to connect to God or people.

PART 1: I LIKE HOW YOU DEAL WITH DISAPPOINTMENT

DAY 1: PERMISSION TO GRIEVE

Let's start out with a confession: One of my greatest weaknesses is an intense aversion to pain. It's why I failed an online math class in high school. It's why I struggle to workout. It's the why behind most of my failures.

I'm learning that leaning into the pain instead of running away from it might actually be one of the fastest ways to move through it.

You can be both sad AND hopeful.

You don't need to put on a brave face or fake happiness. You don't have to be the hero or the joy-bringer for everyone else around you. You don't have to stuff the pain deep inside.

If you need it, this is your permission to grieve.

Cry. Scream. Feel. Let it out. There is nothing shameful about experiencing human emotions. You get to be human.

In our search for hope in the middle of disappointment, please don't buy into the lie that hope means you can't be sad or hurting or angry.

I don't fully understand why Jesus cried when Lazarus died (the story is found in John 11) because he knew that He'd be seeing His friend alive in just a few short moments. All I know is that He felt genuine, human emotions of grief while also knowing the ending would be good.

I know that it is tempting to want to fast forward this part, but there is authentic joy found in going through life with open hearts that feel all the feels while holding tightly to God. Whether God shows up as the Comforter, as the Healer, as the Redeemer, or as the Breakthrough – He will show up.

My prayer is that you will also show up fully yourself and fully feeling.

GOING DEEPER:

Blessed are those who mourn, for they shall be comforted.
Matthew 5:4 ESV

Ask: Have you ever tried to fast forward grief? What did that look like?

Anthem: I am accepted and welcomed as I am.

Activation: Connect to emotions. Write out a few disappointments you're processing through in your own life. It's okay to feel it.

DAY 2: WHAT'S IN A WORD?

The word "tenacious" kept popping up all over my life in the fall of 2018.

It was the story of Catherine and William Booth that really made me say, "Wow! I want to be tenacious like that!"

If you aren't familiar with the Booth power-couple, they were the founders of The Salvation Army. Not only did they start a nonprofit serving vulnerable communities all over the world, but they also raised eight kids. The way that they changed the world despite so many challenges struck me as absolutely tenacious.

Catherine is quoted saying, "There is no improving the future without disturbing the present."

This tenaciousness inspired me to seek it out for myself. At the time, I was wrestling with crippling disappointment that made it hard to raise my eyes above the mess to see what God was wanting to do. I was distracted by my disappointment.

Please, don't waste your life being distracted by disappointment.
Don't quit too soon.

I cannot imagine how the world would have been different if Catherine Booth had decided that she should keep quiet because she was a woman. I can't imagine how it would have looked if she was jealous of her husband's time or energy spent for God rather than joining him in the adventure.

She gave herself fully to God and she changed the world.

We aren't all called to start social reform movements that revolutionize prison systems and poverty prevention programs. But we are all called by God to make an impact for His glory and the good of people.

We are all called for a greater purpose that will take sacrifice and resilience. It won't always be easy. We will want to quit.

Friend, we get to be tenacious. We get to cling tightly to hope, to faith, to a belief that will take us where cynicism cannot. We get to keep moving forward.

GOING DEEPER:

As for us, we have all of these great witnesses who encircle us like clouds. So we must let go of every wound that has pierced us and the sin we so easily fall into. Then we will be able to run life's marathon race with passion and determination, for the path has been already marked out before us.
Hebrews 12:1-2 TPT

Ask: What in the present are you willing to disturb to change the future?
Anthem: I am tenacious.
Activation: Journal about what tenacity means to you.

DAY 3: YOUR EDUCATION,
NOT YOUR IDENTITY

The grief and chaos of my parents' divorce built up and spilled out all over my life. It specifically showed up in my life as a crippling anxiety disorder.

I realized from the beginning of my healing journey that this was going to be a process.

In the depths of my spirit, I heard the whisper of God's voice say, "You need to learn to deal with your pain so when you face hard things in the future, you know what to do. Only then you are able to help others."

This helped me work through hours upon hours of counseling, journaling, reading, praying, and doctor's visits with a vision. I wanted a solid life foundation and tools to help others.

Once, an older friend that I respect was praying for me and asked God about my mental health diagnoses. She knew they weren't meant to be my identity, but what was their purpose?

The answer she received is, "They are your education."

The things that come against us aren't an identity, they are an education. The awful doesn't define us, it prepares us.

We get to take what we learn in the dark and bring it to others who are sitting right where we were. We get to multiply the same comfort that we've received and it becomes more when shared.

The peace you've received isn't just for yourself. The breakthrough you've seen isn't meant to end with you. The joy you carry isn't designed for containment.

Freely receive and freely give. Your life education is enough to qualify you.

GOING DEEPER:

He always comes alongside us to comfort us in every suffering so that we can come alongside those who are in any painful trial. We can bring them this same comfort that God has poured out upon us.
2 Corinthians 1:4 TPT

Ask: When have you been comforted by someone else's story?

Anthem: I am comforted to be a comforter. _____ is an education, not my identity.

Activation: Share a story of what you've been through with someone today. Even if it's just on social media, be willing to be open for the sake of someone who might really need it.

DAY 4: HE IS THE HEALER

I wasn't really looking for healing.

It was during a time of worship where I was focused on Jesus. In a moment of connection I could picture Jesus asking me, "Are you ready to be healed of anxiety?"

My heart said yes, surprised by the timing but hungry for the breakthrough. In that moment, it felt like the anxiety was being pulled out of my body. It was the same shaking as a panic attack, but it didn't feel like it was overtaking me, instead it felt like the anxiety was leaving.

God supernaturally healed me of panic attacks.

What does that mean? I totally had the same question. There was a little fear it. What if I tell people I'm healed and I have another panic attack? Does this mean I'll never be nervous or scared or stressed again?

No, I still still experience moments of anxiety.

Here's what's changed: Anxiety does not have the power to control me. Instead, I've found healing and authority over fear while also learning to tune into my body and listen to the physical symptoms as "check engine lights" going off.

I still have normal stresses of life. I still have to fight fear daily. I still have to choose peace when everything feels chaotic.

But I'm free from panic attacks and the pathological presence of anxiety's grip on my body and life. There was a tangible, physical thing that happened within my body that I can't deny.

God can heal in a moment. God can heal in a process. God can heal using medicine and doctors and counselors and chiropractors. God can heal using prayer and scripture and worship and pastors.

Let's embrace it all. Let's keep our hearts open to whatever way God shows up.

This story of what God has done in my life is not meant to shame you if you aren't experiencing Him in the same way.

I just want you to know this: Anxiety isn't a life sentence. Depression isn't a life sentence.

Whether you choose to see it as "in remission" or "healed," that's not really the point. No matter what you are facing, there is a Healer eager to help you. You might be learning to walk out of the woods one baby step at a time. You might have one moment that changes everything.

Jesus is present and He IS a healer by nature. Keep seeking Him. Keep your eyes on the one you love and you might be surprised what happens.

GOING DEEPER:

Yes! Yahweh my healer has heard all my pleading and has taken hold of my prayers and answered them all.
Psalms 6:9 TPT

Ask: Where do you need healing?

Anthem: Jesus is the Healer. I am invited into His healing.

Activation: Close your eyes and picture Jesus physically present with you. What does He have to say?

DAY 5: BREAK OUT YOUR BREAKUP SONGS

When I finished the final test in my last math class in high school, I drove home cranking the music in my car. "WE ARE NEVER EVER EVER GETTING BACK TOGETHER!"

I viewed math as a bad boyfriend that I was finally ready to shake off, Taylor Swift style.

In college, I finally ended things with a boy who had strung me along and wore a big chunky red sweater while sitting outside on a chilly fall day. It felt so poetically right that I dubbed it my "breakup sweater."

Grab your breakup sweater. Blast your Taylor Swift. Get out your Ben & Jerry's ice cream. It's time to break up with being a victim.

Yes, bad things have happened to you. Yes, it's good and healthy to grieve. Yes, you might have actually *been* a legitimate victim.

But you can't stay a victim if you want to see a victory.

The most powerful people I know have overcome trauma but haven't let it define them. They've recognized the impact, healed from the pain, and refused to be stuck in the label of a victim.

When we move from the mindset of "I am powerless and weak" to "I am strong and courageous because of Jesus," our whole world turns upside down.

No longer are we held captive by the awful, sad, and hard. Instead, we face life and move forward. We know there is purpose in our pain – that while God didn't desire it to happen, He will bring good from the awful. He makes things new.

GOING DEEPER:

Who shall separate us from the love of Christ? Shall trouble or hardship or persecution or famine or nakedness or danger

or sword? ... No, in all these things we are more than conquerors through him who loved us.
Romans 8:35-37

Ask: Do I label myself as the victim in life?

Anthem: I am a victor, not a victim. I am more than a conqueror.

Activation: Evaluate where a victim mindset might have impacted your life.

DAY 6: THE COULDA, WOULDA, SHOULDAS

Disappointment doesn't just happen in external situations. If you're anything like me, you have plenty of opportunity to be disappointed in yourself.

Overthinking regrets is my jam. From little people-pleasing moments and FOMO (fear of missing out) and doubting my decisions to bonafide big mistakes. Maybe like me, you've laid in bed at night replaying conversations and ways you could have been better.

One moment when the "coulda, woulda, shoulda"'s came in full force was when I was a wedding photographer and my computer and backup hard drive both crashed during busy season.

It was a fluke thing that had tech guys shaking their heads and had me weeks behind in my work.

I *could* have had another level of backup. I *would* have done things differently in hindsight. I *should* have avoided the stress and tears.

That stress built up into not just late nights working, but late nights laying in bed being disappointed in myself. I wasn't ending my season as a full-time photographer on a high. I wasn't as organized as I wanted to be. I was so dang hard on myself.

Are you willing to receive grace? Or are you going to beat yourself up for something that you cannot change?

By all means, make amends for things you've done wrong. Be quick to apologize. Work hard. Own your mistakes. But please, friend, give yourself grace.

Start by simply acknowledging that you can't earn love. You can't earn your worth. Remember that you don't need to rescue yourself. There's a God who is always on the move. He's ready to swoop in and be what you need.

GOING DEEPER:

Some of us once sat in darkness, living in the dark shadows of death. We were prisoners to our pain, chained to our

regrets. His light broke through the darkness and he led us out in freedom from death's dark shadow and snapped every one of our chains.
Psalms 107:10-14 TPT

Ask: Where is there regret in your life?

Anthem: I am free from regret.

Activation: ask for eyes to see what God is up to in the places you feel regret.

DAY 7: THICK SKIN, SOFT HEART

How do we hold space for the tension of life?

We want to trust God to do the impossible. We also want to keep trusting Him when we don't see it happen the way we hoped.

If we're going to be tenacious – if we're going to lean into God with everything we've got – we're going to need to learn how to have thick skin and a soft heart.

Having thick skin is the ability to persevere, not taking offence too personally, being resilient, and displaying grit.

Having a soft heart is staying tender toward God and people, not becoming jaded, and bringing our big emotions to the Presence of God.

A ministry leader once told me that they saw God cultivating both in my life. By no means am I perfect at this. My default looks more like thin skin and a distrusting heart. Yet God comes and puts His stamp on all we are.

It's in that oneness with God that we find the ability to not be disappointed. We realize that life will let us down, but God will never let us down. He is too good to disappoint.

If only we saw the full picture and grasped who He really is – our disappointment would vanish in light of His goodness.

Honest confession: I still have a hard time trusting God is going to come through. I wrestle with trust. I haven't seen the miracles that I've prayed and prayed for. Yet...

Friend, I pray that God cultivates in you that thick skin that enables you to keep going alongside a soft heart that is open to Him. Get messy in His presence. Let all those feelings of disappointment be unleashed in prayer.

Here you will find that you are brave and courageous.

GOING DEEPER:

Here's what I've learned through it all: Don't give up; don't be impatient; be entwined as one with the Lord. Be brave and courageous, and never lose hope. Yes, keep on waiting— for he will never disappoint you!
Psalms 27:14 TPT

Ask: Which comes easier to you — a thick skin or a soft heart?

Anthem: I am not disappointed in God. I am brave and courageous. I have thick skin and a soft heart.

Activation: Don't quit.

PART 2: I LIKE HOW YOU STIR UP HOPE

DAY 8: HOW TO HOPE

Step one: believe
Step two: doubt
Step three: repeat

I'm being a little sarcastic here. Hope can't really be turned into a three part formula yet when I stop to think about my own journey with hope, it's something that has to rise deep within my soul. It has to come from a place of resolution in my spirit – that internal knowing and confidence that God is going to work it out for good.

Then, I experience doubt when it doesn't happen in my timing or my way. "Was that really God? Did God really say that? Am I asking for too much? How does free will or our broken planet play into this reality?"

Hope. Doubt. Repeat.

Over time, the cycles of hope get longer and the doubt gets shorter, but so far, I haven't been able to fully kick the "it'll never happen" or "what if I screw this all up?" sort of thoughts. When those thoughts come up, the most important thing to do is to bring it directly to Jesus and hash it out.

Tell him why you doubt.
Express your cynicism.

God can take it. God can handle all of you. God isn't afraid of disappointing you.

Sometimes, I have a hard time receiving the hope that I desperately long for. It's almost as if I want things to get worse because I'm hurt and that's easier than hope. Cynicism is easier. Anger is easier. Offense is easier. Apathy is easier.

It's not just about choosing to hope that God will bring breakthrough and things will get better, it's about being actually positioned to receive that breakthrough if and when it happens. Without hope, it's really hard to receive solutions.

We've all talked to a friend who wanted to be upset. They don't want to be given solutions, they want to vent. You might have a practical idea about something they could do to fix an issue they're complaining about in their relationship or career or friendship – but you quickly realize that they don't want to stop complaining.

I've been that friend.

The only solution to when you get stuck in a place like that is to ask God for a change of heart and a craving for hope.

Today, I pray that you crave hope. May it grow stronger and stronger within you.

GOING DEEPER:

God proves to be good to the man who passionately waits, to the woman who diligently seeks. It's a good thing to quietly hope, quietly hope for help from God.
Lamentations 3:25-26 MSG

Ask: Do you want hope? Do you want solutions or to complain?
Anthem: I am hopeful.
Activation: pray specifically for hope to rise up in your spirit.

DAY 9: DOOR OF HOPE

When I was a sophomore in college, I painted words from Hosea on a giant canvas, not knowing how important they'd become. Shortly after, my family fell apart and I felt stuck in the Valley of Trouble (Hosea 2:14).

The thought that God could transform that desolate, lonely, heartbroken place into a door of hope was almost unfathomable.

Yet He surprised me.

When my parents' marriage first started to crumble, I wasn't sure if I could really believe in love and marriage anymore. What I had seen of marriage in my own home didn't seem appealing. I never wanted to repeat the heartache that I was witnessing in my family. Was it actually worth the risk?

At a conference, a mentor-friend prayed over my fear of making the same mistakes as my parents. From that day forward, an inner confidence arose in me that someday I would get married and, yes, it would be good.

Years later, this passage from Hosea was read at my wedding. Today, that verse still hangs up in my apartment as a reminder of a God who turns trouble into hope. He gives above and beyond what we deserve. The wilderness isn't for punishment – it's for renewal.

This is what God does. He pursues. He transforms. He redeems. He is patient with us. He makes all things new.

What God wants in return is us.

All of us. The whole enchilada. He wants a relationship. He wants daily connection. He wants us to love Him back.

This is where heartbreak transforms into celebration. This is where we step into all that God has for us. We find He's all we've ever really needed.

GOING DEEPER:

Therefore, behold, I will allure her, and bring her into the wilderness, and speak tenderly to her. And there I will give her her vineyards and make the Valley of Achor [Trouble] a door of hope. And there she shall answer as in the days of her youth, as at the time when she came out of the land of Egypt.
Hosea 2:14-15 ESV

Ask: Have you seen God transform trouble before? What did it look like?

Anthem: I give my whole heart to God and walk through the door of hope.

Activation: Get away with God. Get quiet. Even if it's only 20 minutes.

DAY 10: REMEMBER

The transition from disappointment to hope doesn't happen overnight. For me, there wasn't this one moment that erased disappointment from my life or made me bulletproof.

The change isn't about eradicating disappointment, but rather learning how to deal with it.

At the start of 2019, I realized something: I was chronically ill.

It took me a while to come to terms with that label when I have friends who have more severe symptoms. Yet, the reality is, I had been facing symptoms off and on since I was 13 and had several actual diagnoses – from my mental health to hormone imbalances.

Once I finally took ownership of being sick, I was able to grieve it. Then, I was able to start the process of hope.

I did make some practical health changes, but even more importantly, I started dealing with my inner world. Was I finding my identity in being sick? Does sickness in some way reward me? What does sickness cost me? What does God have to say about my body?

Hope was slow. Bit by bit, I started speaking life over my body and situation.

Today, I'm not 100% healed. I still have symptoms. I'm still on a health journey, yet I don't see myself as defined by it anymore. The disappointment surrounding my health has faded. I look back and realize how much my mindset has changed.

Don't rush the process. Keep speaking to yourself and reminding your heart of who God is and why you can have hope. God loves us. His compassion never fails. He is faithful. God is enough. These truths are ones to keep at the forefront of your mind. Don't let them go.

GOING DEEPER:

Yet this I call to mind and therefore I have hope: Because of the Lord's great love we are not consumed, for his compassions never fail. They are new every morning; great is your faithfulness. I say to myself, "The Lord is my portion; therefore I will wait for him."
Lamentations 3:21-24 NIV

Ask: Where are you at in your inner work with hope? Are you able to remind yourself regularly of the reasons you have to hope?

Anthem: I will remind myself of who God is and why I can have hope.

Activation: Remember His love and faithfulness by making a little list of who He is and what He's done in your life.

DAY 11: TALK TO YOURSELF

Have you ever burst out into song and it took you a second to realize you were singing out loud instead of in your head?

No? Is that just me?

This is a common occurrence in my life. It happens on a regular basis, especially in situations where I'm alone in a semi-public setting like an elevator. Sometimes, I just roll with it and keep singing and other times I try to catch myself.

What is mostly a quirk - singing and speaking to myself - might actually be a key to stirring up hope.

In the Psalms, David talks about speaking to His soul. He questions what He is feeling. He tells himself to hope. This shows what psychology has now figured out: What you say to yourself matters.

If you've ever been in counseling or taken a psychology class, you've probably heard about "self-talk" being a key component of our mental health.

We often get stuck in negative thought patterns. One of the ways to break out of that rut is to change how you talk to yourself. This is why affirmations and declarations are central to everything I create for you.

What we speak about ourselves, God, and our situations matter. Our mindset matters.

Choosing to speak to yourself with hope doesn't mean denying your issues. It means being willing to examine them. You can acknowledge what you're feeling but not be ruled by these emotions.

It's time to talk to ourselves. Tell your soul to hope in God and give thanks when you want to complain. The results might surprise you.

GOING DEEPER:

Why, my soul, are you downcast? Why so disturbed within me? Put your hope in God, for I will yet praise him, my Savior and my God.
Psalms 42:5 NIV

Ask: What do you say to yourself? What specific negative self-talk is common for you?

Anthem: I will still praise God. I actively choose hope.

Activation: Today, speak out hope over your life. Practice preaching to yourself. Remind yourself who God is and what He says about you.

DAY 12: GOD KEEPS HIS PROMISES

Once I heard a pastor say that "God speaks in the language of promises."

If you ever want a fun Bible study challenge, start keeping track of all the times God makes a promise. It's astounding. I tried to do this while reading through the Bible for a class, but there were so many times that I had to stop keeping track because it took too long to make note of them all.

We live in a pretty flaky culture that can take promises too lightly. From RSVPing "going" to an event on Facebook and then not showing up (guilty!) to high divorce rates, commitment isn't our forte.

That's why I'm thankful for a God who keeps promises perfectly. I have broken plenty of promises – from promises to do the dishes to promises to get coffee soon to some situations with much bigger stakes.

God keeps every single promise He makes.

It's not always in our ideal — I mean, the promise of Jesus took thousands of years to be fulfilled and involved 400 years of silence. Year after year, generation after generation, the Promise was not yet fulfilled.

Then Jesus arrived right on time.

Why was it at THAT time? I don't fully know.

Just like I don't know why God's promise feels delayed in your life. If you are waiting on a promise from God and it feels like it's taking for-freaking-ever, join the club. Quite literally, my online community, The Wild Abide, is full of others who are in the messy middle. We are a safe place to be confused, but also to lean into the truth that God is a little like Queen Clarice Rinaldi — "never late, everyone else is simply early."

Start making a list of all the promises God makes. Find places in the Bible to back it up so you know it didn't originate from your own agenda.

Some of the promises you find may surprise you. Many of them might already be fulfilled through Jesus. Others might mess a little with boxes that you've put God in. Others might seem too good to be true. Others might feel so far off because they're for eternity.

Remember those promises.

God doesn't forget His promises, but the Psalms are still FULL of David recounting the promises the God made with the plea to, "make this real in my life! Don't forget! Come through!"

You can pray that way too.

Your prayers don't have to be nice and tidy, they can be bold and heartbroken and full of saying the promises of God right back to him. This isn't to remind him, but to remind ourselves.

GOING DEEPER:

This is why the fulfillment of God's promise depends entirely on trusting God and his way, and then simply embracing him and what he does. God's promise arrives as pure gift. That's the only way everyone can be sure to get in on it, those who

keep the religious traditions and those who have never heard of them.
Romans 4:16a MSG

Ask: What promises of God are easy to remember? Which ones do you tend to forget or overlook?
Anthem: God speaks in the language of promises. I will remember the promises of God.
Activation: Take any book of the Bible and start searching for promises. Make notes of the promises of God.

DAY 13: THE BRIGHT AND THE BEAUTIFUL

What do we miss if we miss hope?

This isn't just about happiness. Let's think about it. Make a list if that helps you. What are you missing out on if you get stuck in disappointment?

At the end of the day, the biggest thing that I miss out on when I'm stuck in disappointment is the ability to take part in the bright and beautiful things God is doing.

Sure, I might still be going through the motions. I'm probably still mentoring high school and college girls. I'm probably still going to church. I'm probably still reading my Bible. I'm probably still doing the normal parts of my life where God moves.

But I can show up in body and still miss out on actually experiencing what God is doing.

Strength is not just about working hard and hustling. It's not about enduring just for the sake of enduring or making it into a Survivor-style competition of who can hold on the longest. It isn't about white knuckles and clenched jaws.

A true tenacious strength can come from letting go. It's the result of surrender and trust. It's received as a gift, not something we work for. It's a "strength that endures the unendurable and spills over into joy" (Colossians 1:12).

These words weren't written by someone who had an easy life. The author of this little prayer is Paul, who spent years in jail. He was stoned, shipwrecked, rejected, bitten by crazy snakes, and lived with a major unnamed affliction. He knew something about disappointment and enduring.

Yet he had access to a strength that spilled over into joy. He held tight to hope. He didn't miss out on the good God was doing. He got to be a part of it, even when it came at a price.

You get to be in on it too. This is not just for the super spiritual or the leaders, it's for us all. You get to live into that glory-strength that invites you into an adventure of seeing God move.

Don't miss out.

When you are confused and don't know how to access that strength – ask.

When you feel stuck and overwhelmed – ask.

When you are tempted to sit on the sidelines because you can't go on any longer – ask.

When life is really, really hard, you know what to do – ask.

We get to experience the bright and beautiful.

GOING DEEPER:

We pray that you'll have the strength to stick it out over the long haul – not the grim strength of gritting your teeth but the glory-strength God gives. It is strength that endures the unendurable and spills over into joy, thanking the Father who makes us strong enough to take part in everything bright and beautiful that he has for us.
Colossians 1:11-12 MSG

Ask: What do you miss out on if you give up?

Anthem: I take part in the bright and beautiful.

Activation: Go boldly to God in prayer, asking for whatever you need. Don't forget to also thank Him for what you already have.

DAY 14: STAY WOKE

Waiting has never been my strong suit.

Despite getting married young, I remember those single years of waiting and how daunting it all felt. I was keenly aware that at any moment, I could meet my person and life would radically change. At the same time, it could be years before that would happen. There was no sense of certainty.

There are plenty of moments that I'm not proud of in the middle of that waiting – times I wasted complaining or bemoaning or wondering what was wrong with me that boys weren't seemingly interested.

In hindsight, the area of least regret in how I spent singleness was in taking advantage of the freedom and adventures that it held. My favorite memories include spontaneous drives and long flights. When I leaned into not just fun, but actually asked God, "What are you up to here?" I found the most joy.

When our eyes are open and looking for God's goodness, we are more likely to find it.

This is the power that comes from choosing joy. There's this step-by-step process that is laid out in Romans 5 that I come back to during hard seasons – no matter if it's waiting on a good thing or enduring suffering.

Want to move from longing to overflowing? From resentment and frustration to abundance? Want to live in a mindset of having more than enough?

Start with praise. Develop patience. Find strength. Stay woke & on the lookout.

You will find that God is up to a whole lot more than we could ever expect. Keep looking. Don't close your eyes, lift them up.

GOING DEEPER:

There's more to come: We continue to shout our praise even when we're hemmed in with troubles, because we know how troubles can develop passionate patience in us, and how that

patience in turn forges the tempered steel of virtue, keeping us alert for whatever God will do next. In alert expectancy such as this, we're never left feeling short changed. Quite the contrary—we can't round up enough containers to hold everything God generously pours into our lives through the Holy Spirit!
Romans 5:3-5 MSG

Ask: What are you waiting for? Are you alert while waiting?

Anthem: I am awake to what God is doing.

Activation: Make a gratitude list. Try to go beyond the typical big picture things and really hone into the little things that are happening right where you're at.

DAY 15: HOPE IS YOUR BIRTHRIGHT

Hope belongs to you. You stir it up, but you cannot earn it. You cannot strive your way into it because it already belongs to you.

If you have entered into a relationship with Jesus through receiving the free gift of salvation He paid for on the cross, you get in on all of who Jesus is. We trade all of ourselves for all of Him. It's a good trade. (And if you're curious about this, we have a little note in the back about starting a relationship with Jesus.)

Have you ever fantasized about having an unknown wealthy relative and being left with their money when they die? Maybe I read too many books as a kid featuring wealthy aunts or maybe part of the plot of Cinderella Story got etched into my subconscious. Either way, I was always bummed that no one was going to leave me money when they died.

It's a silly and morbid thought, but it's an honest one.

Here's the thing: life with Jesus is even better.

We are given a new life. We lay down our own life and get to receive Jesus' life instead. We are made co-heirs with Christ. We have a beautiful inheritance that can't be touched – it's preserved and perfected in heaven.

Let's celebrate like we already have all that God has in store for us. Let's thank Him with all we've got. Let's make the most of every moment we have here in the waiting because someday we'll see it in full.

I think in heaven, we'll wish that we had leaned harder into the energetic hope that we can only experience on this side of eternity. Someday, face to face with Jesus, hope will be made complete. We won't need to hope anymore because all will be made right.

Today, we get to choose. We get to choose to worship. We get to choose to hope. We get to choose to love Jesus. Let's rejoice in that choice.

GOING DEEPER:

We are reborn to experience a living, energetic hope through the resurrection of Jesus Christ from the dead. We are reborn into a perfect inheritance that can never perish, never be defiled, and never diminish. It is promised and preserved forever in the heavenly realm for you!
1 Peter 1:3b-4 TPT

Ask: Is it hard to act like a co heir with Christ? What does that mean to you?
Anthem: I have a perfect inheritance.
Activation: Spend time praising God for what you've been given.

PART 3: I LIKE HOW YOU HANDLE THE MESSY MIDDLE

DAY 16: MESSY HOPE

I thought I was good when it came to hope. Heck, I was even selling shirts that said, "Get Your Hopes Up" for all to see. I had come a long way.

Yet, one Sunday left me weepy all day long.

A guest speaker came to our church and his wife shared a story about her parents' marriage. Tears filled my eyes as she told a story that mirrored my own in an eerily similar way. Yet she had a happy ending, a great God moment restored her parents marriage after years of prayer.

After the service, I went up to her and we talked about our stories and the power of believing God when all hope seems lost.

I walked out of church that day full of hope, but also full of tears. The thought of praying bold prayers again hurt my heart. There is still so much not made right in my family.

I couldn't stop thinking about the kind of hope that feels terrifying. Hope that is risk after risk after risk. Hope that doesn't quit. Hope that stands the test of time. Hope that looks to the big picture without overlooking the little moments. Hope that is fierce and tough. Hope that invites others into the waiting. Hope that breaks you down and builds you back up. Hope that is tenacious.

That's the kind of hope that I want.

Hope is not weak, even though it may look like it from the outside. Hope is not wishful thinking.

Hope is far fiercer than that. It doesn't always wrap up situations into picture perfect endings.

At the end of the day, my hope isn't in God restoring my parents' marriage. My hope is in God being good. I don't know how this story ends. I don't know what breakthrough or lack of restoration I will see in my lifetime, but I do know a God who works all things out for the good of those who love Him. That is where I rest assured, knowing that the one who I hope in is trustworthy.

Therefore, I can come to Him with all my jumbled emotions, my messy hope, and He can be trusted.

GOING DEEPER:

Meanwhile, the moment we get tired in the waiting, God's Spirit is right alongside helping us along. If we don't know how or what to pray, it doesn't matter. He does our praying in and for us, making prayer out of our wordless sighs, our aching groans. He knows us far better than we know ourselves, knows our pregnant condition, and keeps us present before God. That's why we can be so sure that every detail in our lives of love for God is worked into something good.
Romans 8:26-28 MSG

Ask: What bold prayers have you held back because you are afraid to be disappointed?
Anthem: God is working out all things for my good.
Activation: Write down some bold prayers that feel impossible. You can get messy with God and tell Him how these vulnerable prayers make you feel.

DAY 17: JESUS IS WORTH IT

Jesus is enough. When it is hard and when your hands are scraped and bloody from the battle – it's worth it. When you are hurt by other Christians or even church leaders and you wonder if you even want to follow Jesus anymore – it's worth it. When you are pursuing a dream that seems to be hitting roadblocks and you wonder if it matters – it's worth it.

Jesus Himself is worth any of the crap that life can throw our way.

When we look into His eyes, we see a depth of love that reminds us of what really matters in the end.

I teach a workshop about dreaming with God. It's a joy to lead people through a process of connecting and listening to God's plans for their lives. There's a set of questions I ask about the end of your life: "What do you want to be able to say looking back? What do you want your children and grandchildren to say when you are gone? What do you want God to say when you meet him face-to-face?"

This boils it all down to what really matters.

Enough of the fluff. Enough of the vanity metrics of success or blessing. At the end of my life, I want Jesus to look into my eyes and say, "Well done, good and faithful child." I want love to fuel me.

Jesus matters. Jesus is worth it. Everything else will fade away – the hard stuff, the fun stuff, all of it. What we are left with is Jesus face-to-face. Let's not miss this moment to press in and experience a glimpse of what is coming.

You can't see it right now, but it's coming. It's coming. Your pain, your sacrifice, your heart is not overlooked, but it cannot compare to the future that's waiting for you.

Right now, it's hidden. The Kingdom of heaven is not found in what we can see in the here and now. The Kingdom is at hand and one day, we will see fully. We will experience fully. We will fully know and be fully known.

It's going to be good. It's going to be worth it.

GOING DEEPER:

For this light momentary affliction is preparing for us an eternal weight of glory beyond all comparison, as we look not to the things that are seen but to the things that are unseen. For the things that are seen are transient, but the things that are unseen are eternal.
2 Corinthians 4:17-19 ESV

Ask: Are you living for eternity? What does that mean to you?

Anthem: I am being prepared for glory beyond comparison.

Activation: Journal through those 3 questions mentioned above about what you want your life to be about. 1) What do you want to be able to say looking back? 2) What do you want your children and grandchildren to say when you are gone? 3) What do you want God to say when you meet him face-to-face?

DAY 18: WHEN THE RISK OUTWEIGHS THE REWARD

I let out a sigh of relief when we hit the break-even sales point.

It was the first ever pop up shop for The Wild Abide and I had no clue what to expect. My heart was full when 40 friends showed up and made purchases from our new fall line. We walked away with a slight profit! It filled me with excitement for an upcoming conference I was a vendor at.

The research said to plan for about 3% conversion rates - which means that out of the 3,300 women present, only around 100 would buy. So I prepared what I thought was conservatively.

It flopped.

We made only one third of what we made at the little local pop up. We didn't come close to breaking even on the cost of our products, let alone the booth rental, hotel room, and gas required to travel. It was a brutal letdown.

As my husband drove us home, I bawled. Then I stuffed my face with Chick-fil-A and cried some more. Losing money while working your booty off is a defeating moment. As an entrepreneur, you know in your head that failure is part of the gig, but it doesn't make it easy. You know that you'll find another way to make the money back, but it doesn't make the fear less real.

When you take a risk with God and it doesn't go well, here's what to do:

Risk again.

Ugh. It sucks, but you have to keep going.

Did you try to reconnect with an estranged family member and ended up getting into a big fight? Did you decide to start a Bible Study and have no one show up? Did you open up a new business and it flopped? Did you go on a date for the first time in a long time and were ghosted?

It sucks. Keep going.

Just because one situation was less than ideal doesn't mean that you are on the wrong path or that God isn't going to bless what you are doing. Now, it might give an opportunity for reflection and revision, but it doesn't mean that it's time to give up.

God is not done with your story. You might be one day away from a breakthrough that changes everything. Keep your heart soft and ready to try again.

GOING DEEPER:

You were running the race so well. Who has held you back from following the truth? It certainly isn't God, for he is the one who called you to freedom.
Galatians 5:7-8 NLT

Ask: What is a risk you've taken that backfired? What did you learn from it?
Anthem: I keep going. I take Spirit-led risks.
Activation: Ask God if there's a risk you need to take, no matter the outcome. Take the risk.

DAY 19: WILDLY ABIDING

God used a funny place to start healing the deep wounds I had surrounding marriage, church, and ministry: Las Vegas.

While my parents' church was closing its doors, I was in a summer internship experience in the heart of Sin City. What I learned there wasn't just practical ministry skills, it was how to stay rooted in the Presence of God while pouring out.

We all only have so much to give. If we aren't connected to the Source, we will dry up.

Vegas gave me vision for what it could be like to have a healthy family and personal life alongside a wild life of changing the world. Yet that didn't mean I learned that lesson once and had it figured out.

No, it took me another round of severe burnout before I started to really realize what it meant to abide. Some seasons, staying connected to

Jesus comes easy and in others, you know you're running on empty, but aren't sure why.

Abiding isn't just about checking off daily Bible reading time. Abiding isn't just about making sure you acknowledge God in what you do. Abiding comes from a place of deep connection and partnership with God.

In stillness and in wildness, we are called to abide.

The Wild Abide (the podcast, shop, and online community I lead) was started from this concept that all the crazy things God calls us to do are supposed to overflow from a wholeheartedness within us. Our output is directly tied to our input.

Abiding is meant to be the place we live and dwell. It's about intimacy with God that goes far beyond twenty minutes in the morning or a Sunday service, it is meant to soak into every area of our lives.

Friend, I don't know exactly what abiding looks like in your life – in the daily hidden places that no one sees or in the middle of the hustle and bustle. Yet I know that abiding is not meant to be this tricky, finicky mystery. It's meant to be natural. God wants to show you what it means in every moment of your life.

This abiding turns striving into surrender. It solidifies tenacity within us. It prevents us from burnout. Abiding changes everything.

GOING DEEPER:

Abide in me, and I in you. As the branch cannot bear fruit by itself, unless it abides in the vine, neither can you, unless you abide in me. I am the vine; you are the branches. Whoever abides in me and I in him, he it is that bears much fruit, for apart from me you can do nothing.
John 15:4-5 ESV

Ask: What does it look like for you to abide? When do you feel it and where it is more difficult to sense that connection?

Anthem: I abide in Jesus. I bear good fruit out of overflow of my connection to Jesus.

Activation: Ask Jesus to show you how to abide. Write down what He shows you. Practice inviting Him into little moments throughout your day.

DAY 20: RECEIVE A HEAVENLY CAPACITY

If you feel weak and tired, join the club. If you aren't quite sure how you could be used by God, you are in good company. If you're running on mission and asking questions about how much longer you can go on, know that you definitely aren't alone.

Here's the bad news: You can't do it on your own.

Here's the good news: You don't have to do it on your own.

There is so much beauty that comes from leaning into a capacity and strength that's beyond your own. It's almost as if God breathes into our lives to expand them. He strengthens us when we want to give up. It happens in the mystery, but it's felt and known.

If you're ever worked at a summer camp or have been on a missions trip, you've probably seen this on display in obvious ways. You feel dead tired – a new level of exhaustion that comes from keeping up with ten children in your cabin or doing manual labor while jet lagged. It's stretching. Yet somehow, the strength comes beyond what you thought you were capable of.

The crazy might catch up with you eventually and you definitely need rest, but the reality is, you are able to do more than you think.

This isn't striving or hustle or working for your worth, this is actually about stepping into a strength that is rooted in the Presence of God.

The cost is that you lay down your own agenda and desires in this trade. His strength for ours. His capacity for ours. His love for ours. We lay it all down and He gives it back in a way that's beyond our human logic or reason.

Take this as a challenge – put yourself in a position that stretches your capacity and strength. Choose to find a situation to be tenacious and keep going.

This doesn't have to be working at a summer camp or going on a missions trip, but it could be.

Maybe you're beyond your capacity when talking to a homeless person or adding in volunteering in the middle of a crazy schedule. Maybe it's leading a small group when you don't feel smart enough. Maybe it's stepping out and sharing your story with someone when you're afraid of fumbling over the words because you know it might make them feel less alone. There are many things you could step into that will stretch your capacity and strength.

No matter the situation, the same truth remains:

You don't have to be good enough. God is enough.

GOING DEEPER:

Yet we don't see ourselves as capable enough to do anything in our own strength, for our true competence flows from God's empowering presence.
2 Corinthians 3:5 TPT

Ask: When was a time you were stretched beyond your capacity?
Anthem: I am strengthened by God's empowering Presence.

Activation: Close your eyes and ask God where you're trying to do life in your own capacity. Then ask Him how to be stretched beyond yourself and step out into his capacity.

DAY 21: REST, DON'T QUIT

The desert is dry. Duh. But, you have no clue how dry until you try to go on a run at 3pm in the summer.

When I was an intern in Las Vegas, a girl I lived with convinced me to go for a run on a 90-plus degree day. I learned the hard way that this will suck any and all moisture from your lungs until you're like Spongebob begging for water. Never again.

It gave me a whole new framework for being dead tired and wanting to give up. Now I can better recognize that I've emotionally felt like I was running in the desert dozens of times.

While I've never seen God supernaturally provide me with the ability to run without getting tired (but that'd be nice), I've seen Him show up for me when I was spiritually and emotionally spent.

The crazy thing is that so often, that renewed strength that's promised to us comes from a place of rest. We wait. We stop relying on our own ability to make it through and instead receive undeserved kindness that compels us.

Slow down enough to keep going.

When you rest, you get the rest.

I don't know about you, but I want to be someone who walks through life without giving up. I want divine strength. I want to be able to keep going when things are really hard or when I'm just spent.

Day by day, I'm learning that perseverance comes when I'm willing to run with God. When I go back to these promises He makes and remembering that His will is good, I am able to come into alignment. From that place of alignment, I'm able to go farther and faster than I could have imagined.

The same is true for you.

GOING DEEPER:

He empowers the feeble and infuses the powerless with increasing strength. Even young people faint and get exhausted; athletic ones may stumble and fall. But those who wait for Yahweh's grace will experience divine strength. They will rise up on soaring wings and fly like eagles, run their race without growing weary, and walk through life without giving up.
Isaiah 40:29-31 TPT

Ask: Where are you feeling tired right now in life? Where do you need God to give you that boost and renew your strength?

Anthem: I am full of Divine strength and grace. I'm not going to give up.

Activation: REST. Find a way to block off rest in your calendar – start with small chunks of time if this overwhelms you. Even 10-15 minutes will help!

DAY 22: GOD ISN'T WORRIED ABOUT YOU

When I first read Ephesians 2:7 in the Message, I was in college and feeling all the pressure to figure out my life. Where should I intern? What would I do after graduation? Where do I want to be long term? How do I get there? Why do I feel behind when I'm not even 21?

Can you relate?

Yet I came across this verse and it reassured me – God has me where He wants me. He's not in a rush. He has plenty of time. He's got this.

God cares a whole lot about you. He notices every dang detail. He hurts when you hurt. Jesus himself is the king of empathy. This is not about being careless or unbothered.

God isn't worried about you because He's got this.

Whatever situation feels impossible right now, it doesn't phase Him. He's not scratching His head wondering what to do. He's never out of control.

He's never fearful or worried that maybe you'll screw things up so badly that He won't be able to fix it.

We're worried. We're freaked out. It's human.

Yet rest assured that God is not worried.

Fear is not in His nature because God is love and love casts out all fear.

Rest deeply in the knowledge that someone knows what's going on and where you're going. Even better news? That Someone can be trusted.

GOING DEEPER:

Now God has us where he wants us, with all the time in this world and the next to shower grace and kindness upon us in Christ Jesus.
Ephesians 2:7 MSG

Ask: What are you worried about?
Anthem: I am right where I'm supposed to be. God is not worried about me.

Activation: Ask God for His perspective on what worries you. Write down what you hear.

DAY 23: THE EMPATHY OF JESUS

Have you ever felt like Jesus doesn't understand what you're going through?

Even when I know in my head that Jesus can relate to my pain, in my heart it's still easy to act like an angsty teenager who believes her parents just, "don't understand."

I've been angry at God plenty of times in my life. I'm not afraid to challenge and wrestle and ask questions. I try to bring my full emotions to God without holding back because He knows it all anyway.

The most angry I've been with God was probably five years into unanswered prayers. It wasn't just anger about the pain I was experiencing with my family, it was the frustration that came from feeling like the situations got worse, not better. I thought we were supposed to be healing, I thought God was supposed to be restoring.

Yet here we were, still hurting.

That's the thing about divorce – it's a slow, painful death that you keep living years after the ink on the papers dries.

I remember being in Chicago at a ministry training and getting a text from my mom with some sort of new drama surrounding potential custody battles or something of that nature. Here I was, trying to love people well, and I still couldn't escape the suck of life.

I ended up opening up that weekend and crying in the middle of a room full of women leaders. That's not something I'm usually on board for. Yet I knew that I could either embrace Jesus, remembering that He gets me, or close my heart off from coming close.

Coming close brought peace.

We have a decision – are we willing to accept the empathy of Jesus or are we going to isolate?

While He lived on earth, Jesus knew pain. He was called "man of sorrows" (Isaiah 53:3), and it's said that he was well acquainted with grief. He experienced betrayal and abuse. He was sinless, yet dealt with all of the crap that comes from living on a broken planet with broken people.

That's the Jesus who gave it all for us. That's the Jesus who's seated in heaven. That's the Jesus we can boldly come to. That's the Jesus who freely gives us all we need.

It's not a Jesus who lived a sterile life in a void. He was holy despite the hard. He can relate to how much things suck sometimes. Jesus is not without empathy.

He's always been about coming close, understanding, and pulling us in.

GOING DEEPER:

Now that we know what we have—Jesus, this great High Priest with ready access to God—let's not let it slip through our fingers. We don't have a priest who is out of touch with our reality. He's been through weakness and testing, experienced it all—all but the sin. So let's walk right up to

him and get what he is so ready to give. Take the mercy, accept the help.
Hebrews 4:14-16 MSG

Ask: When have you felt most alone and misunderstood?

Anthem: I am not alone or misunderstood. Jesus empathizes with me.

Activation: Practice giving empathy to someone around you. Reach out to someone who might be going through a hard time and genuinely listen and hold space for their pain.

DAY 24: I WANT THE REAL THING

Do you remember when #liveauthentic was trending? There were so many jokes floating around the internet about "authentic" hipsters and instagram influencers – there even was a hipster Barbie parody account with 800k followers.

While the word "authentic" became a little cliche and cringe, I think we are craving the authentic more today than ever before.

In a world of fast, cheap, and fake, we want something that is going to last. We've seen too many spiritual leaders fall into scandals. We've watched too many friends walk away from God. We've seen so much that isn't real. It doesn't last.

I don't know about you, but sometimes I've been afraid that my own faith might be fragile too. I've wondered if maybe I'm just going to be another statistic – another imperfect leader who walks away from what she once believed. I've had so much fear surrounding faith and what it means to have faith when doubt is also present.

Maybe it's in that place where we find out what is actually real.

When life is fine and dandy, we don't get to see what we are made out of. When our beliefs get challenged, we are left with whatever remains after the fire. Is it gold? Is it a thin and flimsy imitation?

This isn't meant to shame you. We all have days where we feel like we're faking it. Yet I believe Jesus is inviting us into a relationship that's authentic. It's true, pure, strong, and real.

If that's what you want, then look to this little list of how to cultivate that authentic faith within your life:

- Grow in endurance (or tenacity).
- Don't lose courage no matter how stressful.
- Live a lifestyle of purity and holiness.
- Seek spiritual insight.
- Be patient.
- Show kindness.

- Give uncritical love.

This is not a recipe for overnight success, but for the kind of deep faith that will last for decades. It's the kind of faith that passes down from generation to generation. We go back to the basics and we learn to live it out, a little more each day.

This is worth it. #liveauthentic

GOING DEEPER:

Yet, as God's servants, we prove ourselves authentic in every way. For example: We have great endurance in hardships and in persecutions. We don't lose courage in a time of stress and calamity. We have proved ourselves by our lifestyles of purity, by our spiritual insights, by our patience, and by showing kindness, by the Spirit of holiness and by our uncritical love for you.
2 Corinthians 6:4-5 TPT

Ask: Do you ever fear your faith being real? When have you seen it be tested and true? What does authentic faith mean to you?
Anthem: I have authentic faith.

Activation: Pick one of the practical steps above and make a plan for applying it to your life. Ask God for one action step to begin.

PART 4: I LIKE YOUR VISION

DAY 25: THE BIG PICTURE

The day that I met my husband, I'm pretty sure God was giggling.

We met at Starbucks on Thanksgiving day 2016. He suggested getting an extra shot of espresso in my Americano and we struck up a conversation when he recognized me because my roommates worked with him. I walked away thinking, "Wow, Starbucks employees are so friendly!"

Little did I know that a coworker was planting the idea of dating me in his mind.

If you would have told me that I just met my future husband, I would have laughed out loud.

In so many areas of life, we see such a small percentage of what's really happening. We only get a glimpse of what God is doing. There is this bigger picture that He knows long before we start to figure it out.

God has designed us for glorious living. He lets us play a role in the overall purposes and plans He has on this earth. He saw us first before we ever thought of Him.

We all want to be seen. We all want to be known. It's woven into the fabric of what it means to be human. We crave connection and a place where we belong.

That craving is only satisfied when we find who we are and what we're living for in Jesus.

Friend, I think God is giddy with joy as He sees the parts of your life that seem inconsequential knowing that they are actually life changing. Maybe they are even world changing.

Let's expand our vision for the mundane – from the random Starbucks run to the daily work of showing up in your job, school, or family. It all matters.

Before you ever chose Jesus, there was a place carved out for you. There is a place for you in the kingdom of heaven on earth that only you can fill.

God doesn't want anyone sitting on the bench, we all have a part to play. It's bigger than us.

GOING DEEPER:

It's in Christ that we find out who we are and what we are living for. Long before we first heard of Christ and got our hopes up, he had his eye on us, had designs on us for glorious living, part of the overall purpose he is working out in everything and everyone.
Ephesians 1:11-12 MSG

Ask: What part do you play in what God is doing?
Anthem: I know who I am and what I'm living for. I am a part of God's glorious purposes.
Activation: Ask God for vision for the big picture and your individual piece in it.

DAY 26: INFINITELY MORE

My whole life, I've been a big dreamer.

From being the seven-year-old who confidently told her parents that she was going to someday rescue girls out of slavery in India to the junior higher that wanted to audition for movies, I've always lived in possibility.

Growing up in small towns, that sometimes made me feel odd and unusual. The fears within me ranged from people thinking I'm full of myself to failing at it all and living a "boring" life.

When I read this verse about God blowing our minds, it seems a little crazy. I can't dream too big for God? He has something better in mind for me than anything I could think up? I mean, does He realize how many wild ideas go through my mind? Does He care about my prayers when I feel like they're just wishful thinking?

This is where I wrestle with God. I'm the queen of high hopes and crushing disappointment. I'm an extreme optimist by nature… until I'm not.

My ability on my own to dream big dreams and be optimistic about the future always hits a wall. Reality always sneaks in when things get hard. There always comes a point where I can't do it anymore. The results just seem so different than what I was hoping for.

That is where this truth sets me free: It's not about me.

It's the love of Jesus that we are experiencing. It's the love of Jesus that fills us up and compels us forward. It's that wild, crazy love that empowers us to do more and go farther than our finite, selfish minds could ever imagine on our own.

Love will surprise us. Love will keep us going. Love will be the story told through our lives.

In this place of love, we find out that we can partner with God to change the world, yet the best part is that we get changed in the process. It might look different than we anticipate, but it's better when it's done His way.

You can trust God with your unbelievable dreams and wild imaginations. He's got even better in store.

GOING DEEPER:

Never doubt God's mighty power to work in you and accomplish all this. He will achieve infinitely more than your greatest request, your most unbelievable dream, and exceed your wildest imagination! He will outdo them all, for his miraculous power constantly energizes you.
Ephesians 3:20 TPT

Ask: What dreams are you struggling to be hopeful about right now?

Anthem: I cannot dream too big for God.

Activation: Give yourself permission to dream. Start asking God for His dreams.

DAY 27: WRITE WHAT YOU SEE

Are you a journaler? Truth be told, for a writer, I'm not the most disciplined journaler.

Don't get me wrong, I've been keeping a journal in some shape or form since scribbling about crushes in a hot pink diary in sixth grade. But I've never consistently journaled daily. My journals over the years have become a big mess of prayers, to-do lists, business plans, sermon notes, and endless random ideas.

I share this to break off shame and the belief that it's perfection or nothing at all.

My favorite thing about looking back at old journals is seeing what God was speaking to my heart or what I was praying for. The bigger picture comes into focus with hindsight. Sometimes, I realize that God answered prayers I had totally forgotten about. It's wild to see how it works.

In college, I started an adventure of dreaming with God. I love looking back on what dreams I wrote down years ago. Some stick with me, others fade or change, but the best part is seeing how God weaves the vision throughout our lives.

This idea to publish a 30-day devotional for you is two years in the making.

The heart to see a generation equipped and empowered started more than four years ago.

The dream to see healing in my own heart – to bravely choose things that scared me like marriage and ministry – it's found all over those old pages.

This is why God tells us to write down the vision He gives us. It's so that we can run with it. We can remember what He said. We can wait with confidence.

You have dreams in your heart that are from God. Maybe some of them seem too small to be important. Some of them probably feel way too big to come true. Regardless of your own judgements, write them down.

Write down the vision and trust God with the process.

GOING DEEPER:

And then God answered: "Write this. Write what you see. Write it out in big block letters so that it can be read on the run. This vision-message is a witness pointing to what's coming. It aches for the coming—it can hardly wait! And it doesn't lie. If it seems slow in coming, wait. It's on its way. It will come right on time.
Habakkuk 2:2-3 MSG

Ask: What has God spoken to you in the past that you've already seen come to pass? (Even if it's just in part – celebrate the victories big and small!)

Anthem: I have vision from God. I write down this vision so that I can wait with confidence.

Activation: Write down your vision and dreams! Do something crazy: set a timer for 3 minutes and practice rapid fire dreaming. This is where you have to write down every dream you have for your life as fast as you can. Don't hold back. You might be surprised by what you find.

DAY 28: GOD IS NOT AFRAID
OF YOUR QUESTIONS

A friend told me once, "God isn't afraid of your questions."

At that moment I thought, "Yeah, sure, I know that. No big deal."

It wasn't until months later that the thought kept coming back to mind. It started to stir me in ways that I didn't see coming. If God wasn't afraid of my questions, that meant there was space for me.

I've always been a questions girl. My whole life, I've had a million questions bubbling up inside of me. An insatiable curiosity has gotten me in trouble more times than I can count. I've been known to ask really deep probing questions, sometimes at the wrong time.

When I started wrestling with doubt, the thought that God isn't afraid and maybe even likes my questions became very comforting.

If you don't know something, ask. Get curious.

Don't hesitate to push back. We don't need cliches, we need the truth. Proverbs 25:2 says, "It is the glory of God to conceal things, but the glory of kings is to search things out" (ESV).

This means that when God hides answers from us, it's not to tease us or be mean. It's because there is glory to be found in the search.

There is a beautiful back and forth we would miss out on if we didn't need wisdom and answers from God. If we knew everything, I think we'd get bored. We'd also get cocky and try to navigate life on our own.

Yet we don't know everything. We don't have all the answers. We aren't all wise and all knowing. We are dependent on the One who is. We are connected to the source of all life, all truth, and love.

God isn't hiding to be mean. He wants to be found. He wants us to seek Him out. He wants us to ask our questions. He wants our prayers for wisdom. He's quick to answer. He's a generous giver.

Bring your questions to the table. They may not all be answered, but you won't be turned away.

GOING DEEPER:

If any of you lacks wisdom, let him ask God, who gives generously to all without reproach, and it will be given him. James 1:5 ESV

Ask: What has been your experience with curiosity? Was it encouraged or discouraged in your life?

Anthem: I can ask God questions. God wants to give me wisdom.

Activation: what questions do you have for God? Write them down and be honest with Him about what you don't understand.

DAY 29: BE THE MESSAGE

My friend Emily is the most intentional human I've ever met.

I was photographing a wedding for a friend I met in Las Vegas who grew up about two hours away from me in Minnesota. The wedding was in Wisconsin and I arrived at a beautiful vintage home where she was getting ready and was greeted by a spunky redhead bridesmaid asking me a million questions.

Emily not only asked me genuine questions and took an interest in me as a person, she is the type that follows up. About two weeks after we met, I got a letter in the mail encouraging me. I was 21, super single, and photographing weddings every single week. It was a time of mixed emotions and she spoke into that with kindness and hope.

Almost four years later, Emily is still showing up in my physical mailbox to encourage me and my husband on all of our life milestones. From launching businesses to remembering our anniversary, she celebrates people unlike anyone else.

She is someone who radically lives the message she preaches.

From starting a homeless ministry that simply spends time drinking coffee in real mugs with friends on the street to teaching English in Thailand, she is the real deal.

It's easy to talk about authenticity. It's a whole other thing to actually live that out and it's a journey that we all are on together.

When I look at the first chapter of 1 Thessalonians, I see a few keys to being a living message:

- only value God's approval
- Let the Holy Spirit put steel in your convictions
- Love people fiercely
- Don't patronize or condescend
- Abandon what's holding you back (idols and old ways)

- Embrace and serve God
- Stay expectant

This isn't a checklist, it's a lifestyle. This actually is a way of doing and being that has to be lived to the core, woven into the fabric of your daily life in order for it to have its full effect.

Are you ready to live the message? Not just the message of *I Like Your Tenacity*, though I hope you live it out in beautiful ways that are unique to you. I want to see you live out the Message of the Gospel - of a good God who loves His kids and would move heaven and earth to be with them.

GOING DEEPER:

Dear brothers and sisters, you are dearly loved by God and we know that he has chosen you to be his very own. For our gospel came to you not merely in the form of words but in mighty power infused with the Holy Spirit and deep conviction. Surely you remember how we lived our lives transparently before you to encourage you.
1 Thessalonians 1:4-5 TPT

Ask: Who in your life really lives what they preach?

Anthem: I am living the Message.

Activation: Take time to reflect on the message you want to live. Then evaluate if there's any way that your actions aren't matching up with the message.

DAY 30: WE WILL COME BACK HOME

Home is a loaded word. It holds our highs and lows. It morphs and shifts meaning over time.

Your experience with home might be full of warm fuzzies, but I would bet that there's at least a little bittersweet mixed in. You might have a lot more bitter than sweet.

Growing up, I moved frequently. Even in the homes I lived in for five years, an all-time family record, I switched bedrooms with siblings like they were trading cards. For a six-month stretch, my family was without a home of our own, truly shaking my concept of home as we lived in my grandpa's one room cabin while my dad was between jobs.

Yet nothing could prepare me for the shaking of home that happens with divorce.

During the early days of my parent's separation, it hit me: I had no freaking clue what or where home was anymore.

Home had always equalled my family. Now that was fractured and wouldn't ever be the same.

There was no more "going back home" for holidays or weekend trips. It was now "going to my mom's place." Despite moving in with my mom for ten months after her divorce, her little townhouse just didn't feel like home.

While a sense of home had always been present in Fargo, the rattling shook me back down the core of home. Back to the basics. No more fluff. No more hiding behind walls or even people.

God is home.

True home. Safe home. Forever home.

Home was His idea. The whole story of the Bible is full of stories of home. God creating home for us in the garden. God leaving his home to come down and make his home with us. Jesus leaving to prepare a home for us for eternity.

We are hard-wired to long for home.

While there is a part of the longing that cannot be satisfied in this life, there is an accessible invitation that's available to you today. Come home. Right where you're at, in the deepest parts of your soul, come home.

Be with God. Sit with him. Enjoy life together. Laugh. Dance. Eat. Cry. Celebrate. Sleep. Play.

How? Simply ask. It's not complicated, even though it isn't easy in the middle of our busy lives. This is a get to, not a have to.

GOING DEEPER:

Lord, through all the generations you have been our home! Psalms 90:1 NLT

Ask: What are your emotional associations with the word home? What does it look like in your life to be at home with God?

Anthem: I am home when I am with God.

Activation: Close your eyes and picture God inviting you home. What does it look like? What does it sound like? What does it feel like?

ONE LAST NOTE:

As we come to the end of our journey together, I pray that this month has been transformational. I pray that you experienced God on these pages. I pray that something has shifted deep in your spirit.

Earlier, I told you about my own battle with crippling anxiety and how God told me that He was giving me tools for both myself and for you. This kept me going during dark days where the lies felt too loud to fight.

The stories and truths found in this book have been solidified in my heart during dark days. What God taught me in grief and sickness and depression, I am now speaking out to you from a place of joy. That's wild to me.

Now it's time to repeat the process. You carry hope. You are living the message. You are representing Christ – our ultimate living hope – to a world that is desperate for good news.

What God has done once, He can do again and again and again.

He is excited to multiply His healing, His hope, His tenacity.

It's for you. It's also for so much more than just you. This is for your siblings, your friends, your parents, and the random stranger at Target. It's meant to be contagious - an irresistible grace that is too good to deny.

I want to leave you with this prayer:

God, would you overwhelm with joy whatever has overwhelmed us? May despair disappear when met by your love. You are doing a new thing and yet it's part of the ancient story of what you've been doing since the beginning. We say yes to you. You have our yes. We are all in. For us, for the generations to come, and for the world around us — we say yes to being tenacious carriers of hope. Teach us how. Be with us every step of the way. We trust you and love you.

FINAL ANTHEM

Strong and hopeful,
the dawn will break
and push back the pain.
Come morning,
you will be dancing home,
singing all the way.

BONUS 1: DISCUSSION QUESTIONS

Part 1: I Like How You Deal with Disappointment

- Have you ever tried to fast forward grief? What did that look like?
- What in the present are you willing to disturb to change the future?
- When have you been comforted by someone else's story?
- Where do you need healing?
- Where is there regret in your life?
- Which comes easier to you – a thick skin or a soft heart?

Part 2: I Like How You Stir Up Hope

- Do you want hope? Do you want solutions or to complain?
- Where are you at in your inner work surrounding hope? Are you able to remind yourself regularly of the reasons you have to hope?
- What promises of God are easy to remember? Which ones do you tend to forget or overlook?

- What do you miss out on if you give up?
- What are you waiting for? Are you alert while waiting?

Part 3: I like how you navigate the messy middle
- What bold prayers have you held back because you are afraid to be disappointed?
- Are you living for eternity? What does that mean to you?
- What is a risk you've taken that backfired? What did you learn from it?
- What does it look like for you to abide? When do you feel it and where it is more difficult to sense that connection?
- When was a time you were stretched beyond your capacity?
- Where are you feeling tired right now in life? Where do you need God to give you that boost and renew your strength?
- What are you worried about?
- When have you felt most alone and misunderstood?
- Where are you tempted to take control?
- Do you ever fear your faith being real? When have you seen it be tested and true? What

does authentic faith mean to you?

Part 4: I like your vision
- What part do you play in what God is doing?
- What dreams are you struggling to be hopeful about right now?
- What has God spoken to you in the past that you've already seen come to pass? (Even if it's just in part – celebrate the victories big and small!)
- What has been your experience with curiosity? Was it encouraged or discouraged in your life?
- Who in your life really lives what they preach?
- What are your emotional associations with the word home? What does it look like in your life to be at home with God?

BONUS 2: HOW TO START A RELATIONSHIP WITH JESUS

I *could* try to summarize the entire story of the Bible into a few paragraphs, but instead, I'm going to keep this simple.

When Jesus asked people to follow Him, His invitation was, "Come and you see." (John 1:39)

His invitation hasn't changed. He wants you to come and get to know Him - see who He is and how He does things. Get curious. Keep your eyes open.

A great place to start is in reading through The Gospels - which are the first four books of the New Testament that tell the story of Jesus (Matthew, Mark, Luke, and John). In those words, you can get to know Jesus for yourself. My challenge is to take pauses as you read to close your eyes and imagine yourself the stories, following Jesus and seeing His story unfold.

Instead of a scripted prayer to commit your life to Jesus, this is a summary of the invitation He offers:

> Come to me. Trade your sin for my abundant life. Repent from a place of sincerity and receive the fresh start that comes from forgiveness. Let me heal you from the inside out. Let me show you how much I love you. Let's do life together - transformed and sustained by the power of my Spirit alive in you. I love you. I've already given everything just to be with you. Come to me.

Do you have more questions? My inbox is always open.

"Let me now remind you, dear brothers and sisters, of the Good News I preached to you before. You welcomed it then, and you still stand firm in it. It is this Good News that saves you if you continue to believe the message I told you— unless, of course, you believed something that was never true in the first place.

I passed on to you what was most important and what had also been passed on to me. Christ died for our sins, just as the Scriptures said. He was buried, and he was raised from the dead on the third day, just as the Scriptures said."

2 Corinthians 15:1-4 NLT

ACKNOWLEDGEMENTS

Thank you to everyone whose tenacity made this book possible.

Caleb, thank you for believing in me and the call of God on my life. You've pushed me to keep going when I've wanted to give up - not just in writing, but in life. You have sacrificed in countless ways to make this book happen – from cooking dinner when I'm on a deadline to designing the cover. I would not be here without you. I love you

Katie, you are an answer to prayer. Thank you for pushing me to think, believe, dream, and work better. Your wisdom and encouragement change the world.

Kara, thank you for editing my words and holding me accountable to finish the dang thing. Every writer needs another writer friend and I'm so thankful that I found mine in the dining center freshman year.

Sunday, you inspire me. I like *your* tenacity. Thank you for all that you contributed to this book.

You answered my many questions, listened to my verbal processing, and so much more.

To all my friend who have prayed and encouraged me while writing - Fate, Carl, Sophia, Lia, Kristin, Sage, Emily, Paige, Grace, and more - thank you.

To my family - thank you for letting me tell a small part of our story on these pages. No one else will understand where this message came from quite like you. I love each and every one of you very, very much.

Wendy, thank you for keeping me sane and for walking with me through dark valleys and bright peaks. Counseling has changed me for the better.

Last, but not least – thank you, Jesus!
This is because of you and for you.

THE AUTHOR:

Olivia Alnes is on a mission to see young women know Jesus and live vibrant lives of wholeness and impact. She is the founder of The Wild Abide, a community that she serves through events, an online shop, and a podcast. She mentors college students and helps her husband Caleb lead a youth ministry at Burning Hearts Church in Fargo, ND. In her spare time she enjoys eating snacks in the bathtub.

For contact information and additional resources, visit: www.thewildabide.com